Public.

Open.

Space.

Kate Larsen (she/her) is a writer, arts and cultural consultant based on Kaurna yerta in Tarntanya/Adelaide. Her work has been published or commissioned by *The Relationship is the Project, Meanjin, Overland, Kill Your Darlings, voice & verse* and anthologies, magazines and arts organisations across Australia, Asia and the United Kingdom. As one of Australia's best-known social media poets, her alter ego Katie Keys wrote and posted a daily #tinylittlepoem for over a decade.

In 2018, Kate undertook an Asialink Arts Creative Exchange to the Hong Kong Arts Centre, where she started working on *Public. Open. Space.* A lapsed Western Australian, the home of Kate's heart is Kinjarling/Albany on Menang Noongar boodjar in south-west WA.

larsenkeys.com.au | @katelarsenkeys

Public.
Open.
Space.

Kate
Larsen

 FREMANTLE PRESS

This collection is about power and abuse of power, control and how it is resisted, protested and endured. It includes references to gendered harassment and violence, stalking and murder, internet trolling, political overreach, human rights abuses and censorship. Please take care.

For the people of Hong Kong – in solidarity.

For the people of the Kaurna, Noongar, Wodi Wodi, Yuin and
Gabrielino Tongva lands on which this book was made –
with respect, gratitude and acknowledgement that
those lands were never ceded.

To those who've found safety, community and voice on the
internet, and to those for whom it continues to be unsafe.

And for my partner and my family – with all of my love.

Contents

Whose space is it, anyway?

I AM < on identity, poetry and place >

I am a resident of the internet.

My professional, personal and creative lives all take place primarily online.

Remote and networked, the internet has become my means and my muse. My work is there, my family, my practice as a social media poet now more than a decade long.

In the digital space, I can join conversations bigger than my younger, country-town self ever dreamed – though it was in Kinjarling/Albany where I first entered a room filled with the first computer I'd seen, first heard a dial-up modem's awkward call.

Online, I can listen to those who didn't write the history books my teachers taught us from at school, and learn from those previously denied their voice. I can enjoy at least the impression of freedom of speech, and attempt to shake off the restrictions and expectations of place. Like Chinese artist Ying Miao,[1] the internet feels like home.

Wadjella yorga / Pinti ngangki: non-Indigenous woman, white foreigner
(Noongar / Kaurna)
Gweilo: white foreigner (English approximation of Cantonese, as used in Hong Kong)

As I worked on the poems that would become this collection, I thought a lot about positionality, about the words I use to describe myself.

The words that I inherited: Kate from an English grandmother, Larsen from a Norwegian grandfather.

The words that I co-opted: Keys from my partner, borrowed for my poetry, but also from the keyboards from which that poetry comes.

The words I choose to relate to or against: the 'non' verbs, the 'new' verbs. The words I discard – tentative, careful, poised on context's edge.

The words of place and history: born on Menang Noongar boodjar in south-west Western Australia, Kinjarling/Albany is the home of my heart. Living now on Karna yerta in South Australia, Tarntanya/Adelaide is the home of my current situation, my electoral registration, my partner, my books and my bills.

In both, I am non-Indigenous, whitefella, settler-colonist. I try to sit lightly, with respect, aware of my prints on the never-ceded soil.

In Hong Kong, where I began this collection, I was gweilo or 'ghost woman', and renamed Jì Lìchén (紀麗晨) or 'era of the beautiful morning', a Putonghua naming gift from my Hong Kong Arts Centre colleagues.

Shī rén (詩人): *poet (Putonghua/Mandarin)*

Wǎngluò shīrén (網絡詩人): *internet or network poet (Putonghua/ Mandarin)*

Méiyǒu dìfāng (沒有地方): *no place (Putonghua/Mandarin)*

Less and less, however, do I define myself by the places I inhabit.

I have an Australian passport. I have a British passport too. But it's rare that I identify with either nationality. And rarer still – in the last decade, at least – that I do so with any sense of pride.

I don't feel quintessentially Australian (South, Western or in general), British, pre- or post-Brexit European. Nor defined by any of the places I have tied myself to over time: regional Kinjarling/Albany; suburban Boorloo/Perth; coastal Walyalup/ Fremantle; a Volkswagen Kombi; Singapore (where I gained the label 'ang moh', the Hokkien word for 'red-haired' used for white foreigners in Singapore and Malaysia); inner-city London; Naarm/Melbourne; Tarntanya/Adelaide; or – for six weeks at the end of 2018 – Wan Chai, Hong Kong.

I am proud to have been born on Noongar land, if not of it. I am grateful for the welcome I've received on all the lands I've visited since then. And I'm conscious of the privilege of mobility and choice. So, how can someone so blessed with places feel more connected to digital than physical space?

Perhaps it comes from my embarrassment at Australian and British politics. My aversion to nationalism and how it is increasingly expressed. My tentativeness as a product and beneficiary of settler-colonialism, endemic racism and xenophobia. I suspect it's a little bit of all of the above. But if my nationality doesn't define my identity or poetry, my nationality-less-ness may do.

More and more, I define myself by placelessness. Like the term coined by US critic Barbara Pollack, perhaps I am 'post-passport'.[2] More netizen than citizen. No place and every place. Global and local both at the same time. As this third space evolves, perhaps it's evolving us too.

I (DO NOT) WRITE < on inspiration and appropriation >

At the end of 2018, I flew eight thousand kilometres from ADL–SYD–HKG to become poet in residence at the Hong Kong Arts Centre, one of the final recipients of an Asialink Arts Creative Exchange with the support of the South Australian Government through Arts SA.

My heart beat faster at the privilege of six weeks of immersing myself in poetry and a city so different to my own current home, and at the first sight of the extraordinary building from which I was to work. I started to record my impressions of those first few jet-lagged days.

What we observe
as other:
stranger still
in stranger streets.

And then I stopped. I thought. I hesitated. I resisted the urge to write more.

'Kate vs Hong Kong', those first poems seemed to cry. 'Kate's experience' vs '[insert other experience here]'. Poems about me as 'onlooker'. Poems about the strangeness of this other-place (which were inherently othering, too).

This was not my first trip to China or Hong Kong. I had holidayed in Wan Chai in 2005, and spent a week in Beijing in 2014 as poet in residence for the Marco Polo Festival of Digital Literature. Thinking back, I realise much of the work I made on that residency existed in this reactive space. I wrote poems with me at their centre, rather than the edge where I belonged, someone just passing through. Poems that were surface-level impressions of place.

'It's boring for us,' one of the speakers at The Big Picture conference at Nanjing University said during my visit to Beijing. 'The artists who do the same thing: bicycle, bathroom, pollution. We don't want to work with the same ideas.'

I looked down at my notebook, where I'd scrawled my impression of a hutong public toilet from the evening before, and covered the page with my hand. Even if I wasn't doing poetry 'wrong', I certainly wasn't adding much of interest or value beyond a personal poetic account.

That was fair enough, I guess, for my first immersive writing experience in Asia. In just a week in Beijing, it was hard to push past first impressions – itself offering a useful observation about international residencies, and the sort of work that comes from such short-term engagements with place.

Does this make any residency that takes place in a community an artist isn't part of inherently colonialist? There is an irony in the term 'residency' itself, given the model inserts non-residents into *not-their-own-space*. And residencies display other colonialist traits, such as occupying space and exploiting language, landscapes and icons for their own or their host's outcomes.

'If your curiosity only takes you to exoticising your space, then I think that's very narrow,' Hong Kong poet Nicholas Wong says. 'These kinds of imagery have already been exhausted after all these years. The shoe-shining boys in Central 80 years ago and those on Chater now are the same – what's the point of writing it when there's no reinvention of perspective? When there's no new angle, is there value for it to remain in the literary circle?'[3]

Who was I to think that my interpretations would be of any interest? What was my angle except [insert artist here]? Who was I to add one more gweilo commentary to an already over-saturated field?

I had applied for the residency during a break between full-time work running Writers Victoria in Naarm/Melbourne and a new life of writing and consulting 750 kilometres west in Tarntanya/Adelaide. My motivation at the time was less about *place* and more *not-this-place*, the desire for an experience away from the familiar to kickstart my return to regular creative practice.

I came to learn

to find new words

to eat

to read

to walk these streets

to seek

to sweat

to find.

On my arrival, however, I was immediately overwhelmed by the Hong Kong-ness of Hong Kong. Surprised by the street art, delighted by the food, enchanted by the place, pace and queues-for-all-occasions, in love with the double-decker 'ding ding' trams, awed by the scale and weight of a vertical city forcing itself up and out from ever-more-reclaimed land, and the ways its premium public spaces were shaped, used and controlled.

I had brought so many assumptions along with me to Hong Kong: conscious and subconscious, significant and small. Some were quick to fall away: like how I wouldn't find good coffee (thankfully wrong). Other assumptions took more time to unpack: like how much you can 'get by' without the language (and how contested that language space can be); how censorship can actually encourage creativity; and the impact Hong Kong and Chinese politics have on their literature and art.

Even to me, as an outsider, there was a sense that things were changing, and changing incredibly fast. In 2018, the city was in the tense lull between 2014's Umbrella Movement and the coming rebellion of 2019–20 against new extradition and 'national security' laws. Locals felt the 'one country, two systems' relationship between China and Hong Kong was being eroded – twenty years before the agreed date. The final Hong Kong bookshop selling titles banned in China had recently closed, and the city had just rescinded the visa of a Hong Kong-based international journalist for the first time.

To this, I was an observer, not an authority. Six weeks in Hong Kong were barely enough to glean the slightest understanding of Hong Kong or Chinese politics or poetry culture (even if it was a significantly deeper experience than the week I had spent in Beijing).

Could the difference between an artist-centric, voyeuristic residency and a broader cross-border exchange be simply a matter of time (and the funding needed to make that time possible)? At their best, residencies provide a unique opportunity for shared understanding – particularly for those with the time and inclination to go deeper, look beyond.

I WRITE < a tentative approach >

I had no appetite to write yet another white author's colonial (mis)interpretation, or insert myself into a story that wasn't mine to tell – even if I could empathise with the combination of inspiration + limited time that I'm sure has contributed to this field.

'People wanted to understand,' author Henry Wei Leung writes. 'Yet I can't help remembering the [overseas visitors] I met, who told me with a perversely excited pride just after they had arrived, that finally, finally, they understood what it meant to be a minority. They were quick to forget that privilege transfers, that being foreign is not the same as being made invisible, and that understanding is not a checklist of pains or conquests.'[4]

How could I avoid clichés, colonising or cannibalising stories and images that weren't my own? How could I write against a literary history rather than adding to it? Be an ally to those whose stories had been told on their behalf? What could I, specifically, have to say?

I began by trying to sit with my discomfort and exploring the privileged space between opportunity, authority and voice. By thinking about my identity and who I really represent: who I am, what I (mis)understand, what I have the authority to share. By interrogating the (mis)information and baggage I had brought with me to Hong Kong. And by witnessing a moment in a city that was changing in front of my eyes. A city in which words like these might not be safe for long – with the increasing influence of mainland China affecting language as much as action, and introducing another era of fear of power and resistance to control.

I continued my research, read work written and translated into English from Hong Kong and Chinese poets, writers and thinkers, asked questions, shared and amplified their words. I wondered if I could use this particular moment, this particular engagement, as an entry point for my own creative exploration. Trigger and impact. Inspiration, exploration and response. To take Hong Kong as a jumping-off point, rather than a candidate for subject matter itself. To draw parallels with my own experiences: feminism, activism, protest and digital practice.

And then I began to write. Meme poems, found poems, essays and more. Field notes, research, anecdotes and the wisdom others generously shared. I avoided, discarded or altered poems too closely linked to the Hong Kong context or too far outside my experience. I experimented with the adaptabilities and similarities of language, poetry and code. I found metaphors in computer error messages and social media posts. And solidarity in the (relative) safety of online space.

An imperfect filter. A clumsy attempt. A lesson to revisit and relearn.

I WRITE POEMS < a collection >

All of which led to this collection that, in the main, is not about the city in which it began – though it was, of course, unavoidable that the work not be informed or inspired by Hong Kong. Not just by the opportunity to be a full-time poet within a particular place, but also in it being *not-my-place* and *not-my-home* (even not knowing where that home might be).

The difference of place (which could have been any place) triggered thinking about placelessness, particularly resonant for a poet in the digital realm.

The difference of that place (which could only be Hong Kong) led me to explore physical and digital oversight and control, particularly resonant for a poet physically in Hong Kong, halfway between Australia's open web access and the restricted Chinese 'Chinternet'.[5]

It was helpful to think about placelessness from within an unstructured international residency, to articulate my discomfort and adjustment, and my increasing affinity with the 'post-passport' and 'net artist' scenes. To think about identity and empathy from a place where people felt their identity was being threatened. To consider digital and online technologies at the moment when the loophole that gives Hong Kongers access to it seemed to be starting to close.

I also documented my residency in short-form observational poems that I published on social media. I overlaid text with photographs, words with textures to make meme poems that were poetic responses to the Hong Kong Arts Centre, its programs, and my time in Hong Kong.

These were, I hope, as Dutch author and academic Maghiel van Crevel suggests, not written 'from inside some Orientalist explorer fantasy, but because as globalised as we may hope or fear to be, physical proximity and distance to the things we study continue to matter. As do the dynamics between lingual and cultural selves and others, duly relativised in cognisance of the diversity and the fluidity of where we come from, what we do, and who we are.'[6]

Firmly positioned within the residency context, those particular poems don't have a place here. They were the poetry equivalent of polaroid photos: snapshots or moments in time. Inseparable from the person who made them, they shared as much of me as the places or customs they seemed to be about.

The remaining poems in this collection have drawn inspiration from wherever place is contested, and how control is resisted online and IRL. They were developed beyond my Asialink residency through research and reflection, conversations, walks, events, a bilingual survey of social media poets in Australia, China and Hong Kong, and subsequent residencies as part of Art Works with Guildhouse and City of Adelaide (2019) and Bundanon's Artist in Residence program (2022).

I IMAGINE < a hope for safe and open public space >

The pandemic's restriction of physical travel and almost wholesale migration of artistic and other work online (if only temporarily) has grown the population of the internet further and faster than anyone could have imagined.

As passports gathered dust, we used screens to reach out to each other. As borders and visas separated us from our loved ones – or *everyone*, in many cases – we found each other on the internet. And as we sheltered in place, we connected to global issues in more ways than before – in fear, solidarity and support.

As our place-ness shrank to the size of our homes, we turned to placelessness instead, to the more expansive rooms of digital space. We were joined as residents of the internet, neighbours there if nowhere else. We couldn't go anywhere, but we could be almost *everywhere*.

As a long-time digital local and evangelist, I hope we don't default to 'the way things were before' or return digital life to a lower-rank than on-the-ground exchange. I also hope that – against current trends – our online and offline lives become ever more open and welcoming, creative, collaborative and safe.

Surely, the future lies in the physical *and* (not *or*) the digital, in a combination of the two – in the sort of hybrid engagement and expression that made this collection possible.

It is a collection about this place and placelessness, about freedom and its opposite, the difference between being told 'no' and saying it ourselves, and the choices we make about when to stay silent and when to stand up. About what my Hong Kong residency showed and taught me, not just what I saw when I was there.

Public/Private

Named

We were silent
   Though we were not told to be silent.

We gave them our names
   Though we were surprised when they called.

One by one, we waited
   To be called.

Lost

What's public? What's private?
What's open? What's closed?
What's vanished?
What's silenced?
What's lost?

Civil / Disobedient

'... the disobedience in Hong Kong was very civil indeed.'
– Timothy O'Leary[7]

your hands
are tied /
your hands
are bound

will you: bite
(or) loose your tongue
(or) lose your tongue?

will you: persevere
(or) protest?

will you: ask
(or) take
be im/polite
(or) rude?

will you: sing in tune
(or) discord /
your own song?

will you: dis/believe
(or) question?
will you: stay the same
(or) change?

will you: keep
(or) breach
the peace?

(or) stay
(or) leave?

(or) stay
(or) leave?

are you:
civil? /
disobedient?

are you:

free-ish,
free-er
free enough
(or) free?

Tense

Calculate:
the tense
of <insert poem>.

The sum of:
always here (yet)
always here-then-gone.

The less-defined
by character
than word count:

(a)
plus (b)
plus (c).

By if
(or) not.
(or) product of.

The formula of frequency.
The minimum
of what we need.

The stream
and stream
and stream

and stream
of consciousness
goes on. (And on).

Cell count: sign
of things to come.

Same (or)
more (or)
less than?

What it equals.
What is true.
A valued proposition. False.

The positive. The absolute.
A variance
accounted for.

The average
that's not average
any more.

The Words We Use

When no-one else
is listening (we hope).

The words we want

(and don't want)
to be heard.

Virtual Private Network

We may as well be naked here.

Our every whispered word
between the whisper of our sheets.

Our every morning watched:
a nod in passing,

quiet notes observed.
Each (mis)placed step recorded,

all our choices overheard.
Our every moment counted

and contested, over-served.
The moment when you take my hand.

The words I use when no-one else is listening but you.
The sigh of fallen clothing on the floor.

Barely Lit and Barely Heard

Sometimes shade is all you get
from trying to shine a light.

Sometimes words are spoken
in the dark.

To Varying Degrees

You can speak.
But someone else controls
the volume.

You can ask.
But someone else provides
the words.

You can tick a box.
But someone else will choose
the candidates.

You can write it down.
But someone else will tell you
what you mean.

You can try to hide.
But someone else will place
the cameras.

You can try to run.
But someone else will block
the way.

You are free
(to varying degrees).

Terms and Conditions

Here is where you sign.
Here are the terms,
the layers of words.
Here is the full stop.

Here is where you decide.
To follow or not.
Dissent. Or agree.
To tear apart. Or leave.

To consume;
subsume;
(OR) make
something new.

To bind or break.
To obfuscate.
Consent.
(OR) acquiesce.

To give your digital consent.
Here is where we see
who has complied
and who has lied.

Here is what we carry
in our hands.

[This Connection Does Not Exist]

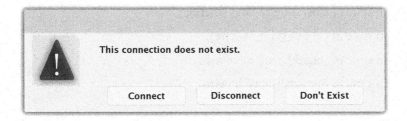

Brave

Brave, in spite of [insert here],

in spite of [insert there] and [there],

in spite of [x] put [y] in [where],

in spite of [blank], in spite of fear,

in spite of her experience [erased].

Obligation

Obligation: comment;
Obligation: hold your tongue;
AND/OR
Obligation: say (OR) do not say.

Trolled

You countered all my narratives –
    had something to say,
    a comment to make
    on each contested line.

Explained my explanations,
    exchanged less conversation
    than repeat / repeat / repeat
    in double time.

You felt the need to add some thing,
    not value, barely more than noise,
    inflamed your own appendix
    till it burst.

She

Trigger warning: this poem is adapted from real online posts directed at
Australian women writers, including depictions of sexualised violence and
misogyny.

She's a [blank].
A [blank]ing [blank].
A [blank]y [blank]ing [blank] or [blank].

I honestly pray
for her [blank] every day.

[Blank], she's ugly.
[Blank]ing.
Bush [blank].
[Blank]o.
[Blank].

If my [blank] looked like she does,
I'd [blank] its [blank],
and teach it to walk backwards.

What a [blank].
Un[blank]able.
That may be why
she [blank]s men so much.
No-one wants to [blank] her.
The [blank]ian [blank].
The [blank] [blank] needs [blank]ing.

Hey, have you noticed:
the good-looking ones

don't pull out
the [blank]in-[blank]y [blank]?

A half-decent [blank]ing
might change her mind.
Me? I wouldn't [blank] her in a nightmare.
But someone should [blank] her a lesson.

She should make more of an effort.
Get a better photo.
A nose job.
A [blank] job.
Get a [blank] drilled in her [blank]
so I can carry her round
like a bowling ball.

She is a [blank]ist.
A [blank]ing oxygen [blank].
A [blank]ive [blank] on society.
People like her are a [blank]y [blank] on this earth.

She should get out of our country.
Have her kids taken away.
She's the reason that her kid will [blank] himself one day.
Has she [blank]ed any men today?

I should [blank] that [blank] in the mouth.
With a face like that I'd be surprised
someone else hasn't
[blank]ed her already.

She should be [blank]ed.
[Blank]ised. [Blank] up and [blank] out.
She deserves to be [blank] [blank]ed
by a pack of [blank]-infested [blanks].

If her husband [blank]ed her,
I'd say "good on him".
But he must be a [blank] of epic proportions.
I'd never let my own [blank] act that way.

She's hysterical.
Unreasonable.
She is not the victim here.
Home wrecker.
Troll baiter.
Can't take a joke.
Lost him his job.

She knows he didn't mean it.
He's a nice guy.
First time.
Free speech, right?

She made him.
She mocked him.
She blocked him.
[She]

#Vigil

For one of the sixty-nine women to be violently killed in Australia in 2018.

I don't speak on my way to the vigil.

I carry my privilege through twilight streets alone. My whiteness, my family, my education, my money, my citizenships (plural), my cis/het-relationship and sexuality-by-default, my gender identity, my (lack of) disability, religion and caring responsibilities, and the size of this small city – safer and softer than the big, hard metropolises I lived in before.

And yet.

Still, I peer into every darkened corner. Still, I cross the street to avoid the nameless men. Still, I know the safety of this privilege is not safe at all – more merely a matter of time.

The park is crowded when I arrive, the ground wet with yesterday's rain. I place a candle, relight some more and burn my thumb on my lighter. It leaves a small embodiment of the bigness we all feel. Another day, another loss, another scar.

Strangers stand in silence. One minute for each kilometre she was hunted through the streets. Our shadows, grief and fury in the dark.

This Is the Change We Create with Our Silence

[   ]

This Is the Change We Create by Being Polite

[   ]

[You Cannot Act]

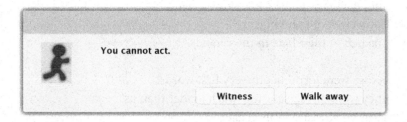

Then They Were More

As we were taking our very first steps,
they'd already taken too many of theirs,
the weight of them bigger,
the heft of their hate in their hands.

As we were forming our very first words,
they were there, shouting much louder than us,
their voices raised full of agendas,
raised full of command.

As we were cutting our very first strings,
and pulling down all of our old scaffolding,
we couldn't see who was still building
or pulling on theirs.

We thought we were many,
but then they were more.

We thought we were many,
but then they were more, they were more.

Weaver

The length of her submission,
fabric read as stories told.

The length of her resistance
in each closely folded fold.

Rules

The rules we break
behind closed doors.

The rebels we can be
when no-one sees.

Smilence[8]

We are tireder now,
and we have stopped our arguing.

Bored of wasting time. Resigned
that some things can't be changed.

Decide: we plan to NOT react.
The system is the problem.

[AND] reacting to the system
is the system's problem too,

[AND] though we're not indifferent,
we won't waste each other's time.

We could reach out, but don't.
Hands sore from being too-smacked down –

like children misbehaving
at the table. Bruises last.

We discard our old placards,
shine a torch into the dark

to find the things we'd lost
or had been forced to put away.

We sit there with our scars and masks.
We offer up our smilence: biding time.

Where Is Your Anger?

They can ask
'Where is your anger?'[9]

They can watch us walking,
and never see that fury moves our feet.

They can see us keep the peace
not knowing what we've grown,

not knowing what we've learned
the hardest way,

between the shock and aftershock,
and what we had to pay.

Our anger can be quiet, in the street.
a space once passed, reclaimed.

Clearer Water

We will wash in clearer water.

We will hold and stroke and turn
each other's hands.

First you for me, then me for you.
A privacy that everyone can see.

And underneath, our new shared skin,
we'll slough off all the things

we thought we'd need,
the things we thought we'd seen.

And later, when the water's poured aside,
we'll dry each other's finger pads,

and carry bowl and towel away again.

Hidden Things

These hidden things
aren't hidden
any more.

Open / Closed

No Admission Beyond This Point

[   ]

[Read Error]

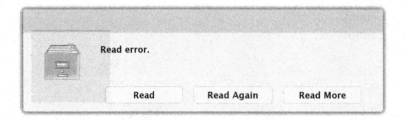

Cannot / Can

Cannot!
Cannot.
Cannot…
Cannot?

Can?
Can…
Can.

Binary

The binary / poetry.

0101010001101000011001010010000001000010011010010110 1
1100110000101110010011110010010000001101111011001 1000
1000000101000001101111011001010111010001110100 1111001

The languages we can / not read.

010101000110100001100101001000000110110001100001011 01
11001100111011101010110000101100111011001010111001 100
1000000111011011001010010000001100011011000010110111
000101111011011100110111110111010000100000011100100110
01010110000101100100001011 1000001010

The codes we use for meaning / making words

0101010001101000011001010010000001100011011011110110 0
1000110010101110011001000000111011101001010010000001
1101010111001101100101001000000110011001101110011 1001
000100000011011010110010101100001011011100110100101 10
111001100111001010000100000011011010110000101100110110
110100101101110011001110010000001110111011011011 1100
10011001000111001100101110000 01010

Do You Want to Continue?

Word search: porn.

> When you send information to the internet,
> it might be possible for others to see that information.

Word search: reform.

> Do you want to continue?

Word search: freedom.

> Don't show this message again.

Choose

Please colour in between the lines.

The lines have been provided for your education.

Please hold tight to the handrail.

The handrail has been sanitised for your protection.

Please select your answer from one of the following choices.

The choices have been made in your best interests.

Please mind the gap.

The gap cannot be removed.

Easy as X, Y, Z

I listened to my lessons.
I read my way right to the edge
and didn't look beyond.

I listened to my teachers.
I learned respect as high as walls
I'd thought they'd climbed so we need not.

I didn't know their versions were
what they'd been told to teach.
I didn't know to ask them.

I didn't know asking
was a thing that I could do.
I didn't know the truth.

File Not Found

After the revolution: a found poem

Something went wrong.
An internal error has occurred.

An operation was attempted
that was incompatible with the current state.

Illegal modify operation.
Illegal command.

The system does not support the specified control.
The request to control remotely was denied.

The attempt to change the system's power state was vetoed.
The attempt to rebuild the hierarchy failed.

Insufficient resources exist.
Function failed during execution.

The requested delete operation could not be performed.
The requested operation was not allowed.

You do not have permission to access.
The action could not be completed.

Negotiation took too long.
This object is not allowed to change.

A potential deadlock condition has been detected.
The process was not ready.

A system that should never fail has failed.
The system cannot start another process at this time.

A system shutdown is in process.
You need to restart.

The system is unwilling to process the request.
Please try again later.

Abort, Ignore, Retry, Fail?
This may take a while.

Run error.
File not found.

[Request Blocked by the Firewall]

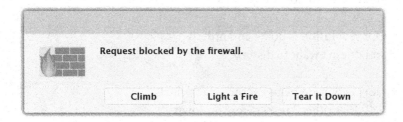

Request blocked by the firewall.

Climb | Light a Fire | Tear It Down

Our Revolution

Our revolution knows when to stay quiet
and is used to not being heard.

Our revolution is polite and orderly
and doesn't want to disturb.

Our revolution helps soothe others' hurts
and dries others' tears before our own.

Our revolution knows how to mind manners
and when to swallow our words.

Our revolution is used to being burned.

Our revolution uses initials
to sell books with less female names.

Our revolution straps down our curves
so they're not used against us again.

Our revolution takes a packed lunch
and is home in time for tea.

Our revolution won't poop on the party
and doesn't want to rain on the parade.

Our revolution is used to taking the blame.

Our revolution is listening.
Our revolution is making a list.

Our revolution is waiting
and won't upset the relatives.

Our revolution cleans house.

[Information Censored]

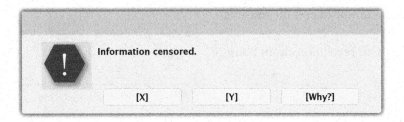

[Requested Value Is Unknown]

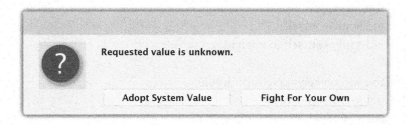

Requested value is unknown.

Adopt System Value   Fight For Your Own

All Things Being Equal

After Nicholas Wong[10]

You will apply,
and apply yourself,
and apply yourself to applying.

You will make yourself applicable,
and in the same form
as everyone else.

You will dress appropriately
and address yourself
the same.

You'll make an appeal
based on your most
appealing features.

You'll propose
something proportionate,
equivocate equivalence.

Your pertinence
in keeping
with the theme.

You will perform
as expected, and be expected
to perform.

You will sign with your initials,
a closely chosen pseudonym,
a preference for fluidity,

a shadowed anonymity
that doesn't mean
you won't return their gaze.

[Save Me]

[The System Cannot Be Changed]

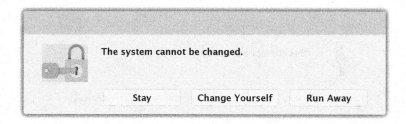

[This Attempt Has Failed]

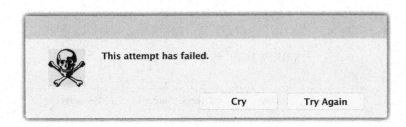

Write Fault

For Victor Mallet: a found poem[11]

[X] has encountered a problem.

[X] could not read.
[X] could not be read.
An attempt was made to log on by [X].

The entry attempt was invalid.

Page fault detected.
The entry attempt has not been found.
The user was not allowed to log on.

The media is not ready for use.

No media is currently available at this time.
The media does not represent a valid medium.
There is no media in the drive.

No library slots are currently available for use.

The library, drive or media pool is empty.
The library, drive or media pool must be empty to perform.
The library is full.

Data error.

Data of this type is not supported.
The data is invalid.

The database is corrupt.

Found infected file.

No more data.
No more data is available.
Could not be saved.

The printer is known to be unreliable.

The printer is known to harm the system.
The printer is not compatible with a policy.
The file waiting to be printed has been deleted.

Unexpected error.

A protocol error occurred.
A request to send or receive data was disallowed.
Please investigate.

Write fault.

Could not be written.
Could not be opened.
Unable to resolve.

[You Are Out of Memory]

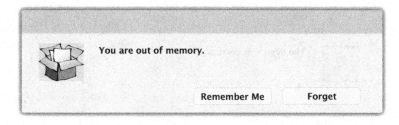

[The System Is Corrupt]

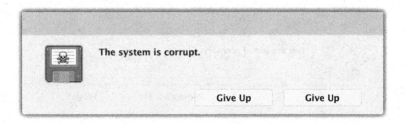

Space/lessness

Connected

Connected.
(Dis)connected.

We are plugged
and (un)plugged.

We are waiting
in the dark.

We are a part.
We are apart.
We are (a)part.

Right or Right

You were a bystander only:
your calendar and motivations clean,

a blinking cursor line, blank screen –
and minding your own businesses

with nothing much to say.
Until the day

the world moved
and it moved you:

bowels and bile and
phlegm and tears.

The choice you had to make:
Step up? Pull down?

The bitter taste inside your mouth.
Triggered, with the gun smoke in your throat.

Triggered, with your finger
on your careful / careless words.

The chance to cheer or witness.
Or the chance to smash or tear.

Not everyone goes down
without a fight.

What's your right?
What's right?

[Safe Mode Not Available]

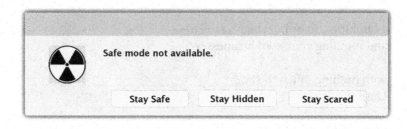

Safe mode not available.

Stay Safe   Stay Hidden   Stay Scared

Absence. Solidary.

I wish I could have
stood there by their sides.

I wish I'd offered shelter,
wiped the tear gas from their eyes.

I wish I'd called a warning,
added my voice to their cries.

I wish I could have held their hands
while they had held their lines.

All the revolutions that I missed.
I wish. I wish.

Transgressed

There is a fault here.
A tear in the fabric.

A stitch once dropped,
unravelled and remade.

A held and mended parcel,
torn and taped.

A pattern mapped
in fragile, fraying thread.

A tapestry unpicked.
Unspun.

Peeled back. This act
of crossed, uncrossed.

A fold.
A cut.

A slice.
So neatly hemmed.

Ness-less-ness

Less than this:
Australian-ness or more?

Less-ness?
Or ness-less-ness?

My X-ness
un-defined.

The nothingness
of no-where

pushed and pulled
like sliding doors,

devices kept connected
and apart, the beating

of my heart the same
in any ness or font or type.

Grammatica

For the Hong Kong Arts Centre[12]

/ The past is hardly simple

The grammar of our histories: unclear.
Who gets to write it down?
Who gets to choose: remember or forget?

Triangulate which past we would prefer,
which choice of dying dream,
select the means of memories,

the backwards view, the scaffolding:
reclaimed, removed, rebuilt and overseen.
The languages we use, the words we find,

the words we leave behind.
The histories – sieved and filtered –
drawn from different pens.

The choices made, selected, changed and lost,
as shaped through paragraphs.
The past is hardly them, is hardly us.

/ The present, hardly perfect

The structure of our sentences: uncertain.
All we wish that we'd forgotten.
How we oscillate: what we can choose and not.

The sting of every paper cut,
the weight of obligation
and creation and regret.

The claimed, unclaimed and counterclaimed,
inched closer to where we don't want to be,
the surface and beneath.

This buying air and emptiness,
what we can move, what moves us
in return, the things we wish would never change.

Nostalgia for the change we think will come,
as seen through smoke and haze.
The present, hardly gifted, hardly made.

/ The future, hardly tenable

The term of all our sentences: unknown,
as seen through telescopes.
Predictions made and lost, predictions hoped.

Continuous. Or palliative. Won't be perplexed
if our best guess goes wrong, the stars
that tell our future hard to see.

A future we can dream of, think of,
craft with chosen words, crossed fingers.
Shape with all our voices carried high.

When activists and art combine to … what?
A language redefined,
and pulled from memories past.

The histories that we don't want to repeat.

Rivers and Lakes[13]

In the context of geography,
we should show each other

how we shaped the water:
moulded, disappeared,

and shortened river's course.
The places where we forced it,

drew a line and watched it dry.
And how the water mapped us in return.

All that fell before. The sediment
it left behind,

the weight it could sustain.
The landlocked place

we claimed, discarded,
spaces that we staked and guarded.

How the water found
and bound us,

bent us to (in)action
as we'd bent its lakes through ours,

our footing too unstable
in the ever-stronger stream.

How we're helpless
in its current,

suspended for a moment
and yet buoyed.

Borrowed

This borrowed space.
This borrowed time.

This history
inflicted
and returned.

Vertical Cities

This not-land
we're claiming.

This space
that we make
out of air.

<3

Have we swapped talk for typing?
Or enhanced it: cyborgs all?
Is code the latest language
of our love?

Freedamn[14]

The freedamn to be found
within the alphabet,
within the words,
the characters we choose.

The words that fall
upon the floors,
the harm that comes
in harmany, freedom in being

slightly less than free.
The words too hot
for writing, burning holes
in what they touch.

The holes through which
yet more words fall,
are lost, are wiped
from memory or touch.

Freedumb

Fake news from real tweets

[SEARCH FOR: #AUSPOL]

The media and politics [are] complicit –
[When] freely given a platform –
[Former Prime Minister Scott 'ScoMo' Morrison
      implored us to] 'pull these merchants of false ideas
      / fake news into line – they are a disgrace' [he said] –
Contradicting the evidence of our own eyes –
His plainly false description presented side by side
      with what actually happened –
[But] 'the PM said …' is NOT journalism –
Media outlets write headlines which make [perspective] –
      NEWS YOU CAN'T TRUST –
      a self-fulfilling prophecy –
[then] blindly repeat Morrison's lies –
      [and don't say] 'today, the PM *falsely* claimed –
[or ask why] 'Morrison makes false claim' is news,
      unless followed by the word 'again'?

[SEARCH FOR: #NEWSCORPSE]

Every news org in Aus – is also complicit –
      [for] spouting false balance and lies –
[Which is why] Twitter stripped News Corp's *The Australian*
      of its 'blue tick' status –
      [before that was something to buy]
A legacy of sensationalised reporting –
[Their] fervent efforts – a barrage of
      false and misleading assertions –
      [often] factually wrong –
The ACCC forensically compiled – yet another FALSE social
media post

by a News Corp employee –
BREAKING NEWS: PAUSE THE PANDEMIC –
News Corp goes full frontal –
    [with] deliberately biased, false
    and disingenuous – clickbait –
News Corp editors have been left red-faced –
    [by] the embarrassing scare campaign –
    [which], since concluded – could not verify false claims –
    [nor] provide data to back [its] bizarre furphies –
The Documents Are Out of Date
    and Have NO Status – [Unproved] –
[But] at what point of blatant lies and misinformation
    can the title of 'journalist' be removed?

[SEARCH FOR: #FOXNEWS]

Don't take the bait.
Trump's plan to overturn the [US] election
    relied heavily on Rupert Murdoch's Fox News
    to propagate his election lies –
[A] massive conspiracy – Fox has claimed in Federal Court
[several times] –
    that it is not news but entertainment –
    shamelessly pushing Trump's big lie –
[But it] didn't come out looking too flash –
Lack of transparency and fibs
    were on the menu –
[And] when there are tapes,
    it's always bad news for the liars –
    [Putin's next in line] –
    [who] change the very concept of 'truth' –
[But it's time to] STOP – disseminating – faux news –
    [and] maybe actually read the information you've been
        referencing.

[SEARCH FOR: #TRUMP]

The [first] night [Donald] Trump got banned from Twitter –
    [he stole] senior aides' phones
    to tweet from their accounts [instead] –
Telling false narrative –
    sowing division –
    supporting falsities –
    [and] lying to the public –
There was no insurrection, [he said] –
    unproven allegations –
    pretending to be real –
[Then @PresTrumpTS was] banned too –
    Which means he was booted TWICE –
    WHAT A [SORE] LOSER –
[The] FBI Deemed Claims False in Less Than a Day,
    Agent Says.

[SEARCH FOR: #MUSK]

Let's not be naïve about Musk –
'I still think Trump should be returned to Twitter' –
    bullshit baffles brains, [he said] –
[Then bought it – twice] for 40 billion –
    [instead of ending] world hunger with that –
    and people lost their heads –
[A] Victory for Free Speech or Online Harassment? –
[Then when] Twitter's acquisition went on hold –
    Elon wasn't sitting on the fence –
    [claiming] most Twitter users were bots [instead] –
[Which led to] defamation – party A claims party B
    said something B knew to be false,
    and the reputation of A was harmed by it –

Truth is a defence –
     Humans are more likely than robots to spread false news –
If A had a bad reputation already,
     [then] that's a defence [too] –
Musk lit up Twitter [again] after declaring he'd vote GOP –
     [when he] realised the Presidency was up for grabs –
     'The left should reflect on why' [he said] –
Using Trump's playbook –
     [he] claimed hit-pieces were coming for him –
     paid off a sexual assault victim –
[So I guess] #FreedomOfSpeech,
     like all our other freedumbs, isn't free.

Analogue

For Joshua Wong[15]

Imagine if we printed
every comment, like or Facebook post,
each stream of Twitter consciousness,
Insta breakfast, TikTok feed.

Imagine all the reams of trees
to re-record our online world,
to document our documents,
ephemera to paper pin.

Imagine then the silence
if it stopped, the written absence of
the words that still go on
when we can't hear.

Perforation

You tear along the dotted line
but something's left behind.
Something's always left behind.

Nothing to See. Move Along.

[   ]

Watermarks

When the rain is over;

when clouds have cleared
and left us
with our more accustomed haze;

when umbrellas
have been shaken,
closed and dried;

when we have cried
our final words,
and wept our final tears;

we will bear
the marks left
after the rain.

Banned. With.

We make our way on (pre)determined paths.
          _ We push _
We hit dead ends. We stutter –
when it's too crowded to see, too choked for clarity.
          _ Turn back _
from where we're not supposed to be.

Banned. With no way forward.
We retreat.

We file ourselves a way into the line. We queue.
          _ We wait our turn _
Stand firm. Apply our body weight into any gaps we find.
We move in ordered time. We grasp the handrail tight.
          _ We hold _
Demand exceeds supply.

Banned. With no clear access.
We comply.

We follow maps and breadcrumbs left behind for us. We mind the
signs.
          _ We hesitate _
Move slowly, thick like blood. We crush
the mass when it obstructs us. Closed off.
          _ Park _
when we're in gridlock, deadlocked, unable to move.

Banned. With busy signal.
We re-route.

Undeterred, we find new tracks, new alleyways.
       _ We don't look back _
We pack and stack ourselves inside. We close align. We set alight.
We climb the walls of webbed and narrow streets.
       _ Adjust the frequency _
We mind the gap. Capacity exceeds.

Bandwidth. No permission.
We believe.

Clictivist

Complicit:
witness
cannot be
enough.

[The System Needs To Be Shut Down]

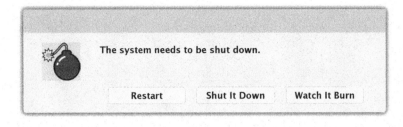

The system needs to be shut down.

Restart   Shut It Down   Watch It Burn

Notes

The specific, positive dedications in this collection are attributed almost exclusively to men, which sits uncomfortably for me in what I hope is a strongly feminist collection. However, it is the absence of other dedications that I hope will be more telling. Many of the poems were inspired by or intended for people who have been oppressed or marginalised, a cohort too large to meaningfully identify. While several were inspired by interactions with and observations of specific individuals, I have deliberately not named them – be that in fear of re-traumatising or re-linking them to ugly words or situations, in fear for their safety, or in an attempt to redirect attention away from targets, victims and survivors and towards their unnamed perpetrators, accomplices and trolls on whom the blame should fall.

1   Ying Miao, 'Ying Miao's Chinternet Mash-Ups and Tech Abstraction at Art Basel Hong Kong 2016', 2016, BAL Productions, vimeo.com/162455923.

2   Barbara Pollack, 'Quintessentially Chinese art gives way to a globalidentity', 2018, *The Art Newspaper*, 14 September 2018, theartnewspaper.com/comment/from-chinese-ness-to-a-global-identity.

3   Nicholas Wong, quoted by Karen Cheung, 'Why Nicholas Wong is "resigned" about Hong Kong poetry', November 2017, Still/Loud, still-loud.com/2017/11/04/why-nicholas-wong-is-resigned-about-hong-kong-poetry/. With permission.

4   Henry Wei Leung, 'Ruins Above Water', *Goddess of Democracy*, Omnidawn, 2017.

5   The Chinese internet (or 'Chinternet') is a government-restricted digital space that filters, blocks or makes many international sites

and communication platforms difficult to use, requiring Chinese internet users to turn to more heavily-monitored local equivalents instead.

6 Maghiel van Crevel, 'Walk on the Wild Side: Snapshots of the Chinese Poetry Scene', December 2017, Modern Chinese Literature and Culture Resource Centre, The Ohio State University, u.osu.edu/mclc/online-series/walk-on-the-wild-side/. With permission.

7 Timothy O'Leary, 'On Anger and Love, in Post-Occupy Hong Kong', Umbrella Movement, September 2016 (Issue 33), *Cha: An Asian Literary Journal*, asiancha.com/content/view/2510/579. With permission.

8 'Smilence' is a rèci (热词) hot-word used by Hong Kong and Chinese writers instead of their English equivalents to avoid triggering banned word sanctions within the Chinese government's firewall. See bbc.com/worklife/article/20180809-chinas-rebel-generation-and-the-rise-of-hot-words.

9 Passerby at the 1978 Harvey Milk commemorative march in San Francisco, quoted by Timothy O'Leary, 'On Anger and Love, in Post-Occupy Hong Kong' (see Note 7).

10 Poet and teacher Nicholas Wong is the first Hong Kong poet to win the prestigious Lambda Literary Award.

11 Hong Kong resident, British national and *Financial Times'* Asia news editor Victor Mallet was barred from re-entering Hong Kong in 2018, weeks after the government refused to renew his work visa in seeming retribution for a dispute about national sovereignty and freedom of speech. See '"Chilling message": Hong Kong refuses to explain FT journalist visa denial', 8 October 2018, edition.cnn.com/2018/10/07/asia/hong-kong-ft-mallet-visa-intl/index.html.

12 Established in 1977, Hong Kong Arts Centre (香港藝術中心) is a non-profit arts institution and art museum in Wan Chai, Hong Kong. In celebration of its fortieth anniversary in 2018, HKAC presented 'Wan Chai Grammatica: Past, Present, Future Tense,' for which the poem 'Grammatica' was named. Curated by Valerie C. Doran and the HKAC curatorial team, the flagship exhibition explored Hong Kong's cultural and artistic identity through the lens of one of Hong Kong's most iconic city districts, Wan Chai. Kate Larsen's Creative Exchange at the Hong Kong Arts Centre was supported by Asialink Arts and the South Australian Government through Arts South Australia.

13 Emerging in Chinese poetry communities in the late 1990s, the term 'rivers and lakes' (江湖) has become a common metaphor for the Chinese internet, which provides particular pathways users may choose to resist, reshape and/or navigate around. See Lin Zhongxuan, 'Internet, "Rivers and Lakes": Locating Chinese Alternative Public Sphere', *Chinese Studies*, 2014, 3: 144–156, pdfs.semanticscholar.org/4f4f/8cdb09493b2cb900617a53fdc07b7263b210.pdf.

14 'Freedamn' and 'harmany' are rèci (热词) hot-words (see Note 8).

15 Joshua Wong is a Hong Kong activist and former politician for the pro-democracy party Demosistō, which was disbanded in 2020 following the implementation of Hong Kong's 'national security law.' Wong was seventeen years old when he became the face of the 2014 youth-led Umbrella Movement. Imprisoned several times for organising or participating in 'unauthorised assemblies', Wong's supporters sent him printed copies of comments from social media accounts while he was in prison. See twitter.com/joshuawongcf.

Acknowledgements

I am full of joy and gratitude to all who made this dream come true.

My residency at the Hong Kong Arts Centre was supported by Asialink Arts and the South Australian government through Arts South Australia.

'She' was originally written and performed for The Hearth Collective's 'Masquerade' at the 2018 Adelaide Fringe Festival.

'Civil / Disobedient' was originally published in Issue 57 of 聲韻詩刊/ *Voice & Verse Poetry Magazine* (November–December 2020): Special Feature 'Home'.

Huge thanks to Asialink Arts, Arts South Australia, Guildhouse, City of Adelaide and Bundandon for the residencies where much of this work was made. Thanks also to Connie Lam, Teresa Kwong and the entire Hong Kong Arts Centre team. And all of the artists, thinkers and writers who spoke to me, wrote about or inspired my research there, including Barbara Pollack, Chris Song, Ernest Chang, Heather Inwood, Henry Wei Leung, Maghiel van Crevel, Nicholas Wong, Tammy Lai-Ming Ho, Timothy O'Leary, Suyin Chiu and survey participants.

To Fremantle Press for wanting to share this work with the world – particularly my phenomenal editor, Georgia Richter, for championing the book from the first early-morning phone call, and for her enthusiasm, gentle-yet-mind-blowing insights, and forensic identification of disjointed metaphors.

To Bronwyn Lovell (without whom this book would literally still be in a drawer), Alex Adsett, Jinghua Qian and Maxine Beneba Clarke for their generosity and wisdom, and to Jack Collard, Laurie Steed, Larry Blight, Barbara Temperton, Bebe Backhouse, Esther Anatolitis, Dominic Guerrera, Jennifer Mills, Sarah Tooth and David Ryding for helping launch my little green book into the world.

To the rest of my online and IRL writing communities, including my Writers Victoria, National Writers Centre Network, Hardcopy and Poetry Book Club fams, Julien Leyre and the Marco Polo Festival of Digital Literature, Stella Young, Ebony Frost and Jade Lillie. To Varuna, for shortlisting this manuscript in their 2020 Publisher Introduction Program. To all the extraordinary, hard-working creators and storytellers who put passion ahead of practicality to make and share stories and words. And to those who love poetry, from song lyrics to sonnets and #tinylittlepoems.

To Jacquie, Jen, Hannah May, Chris W., Casey J., Eric and Brayden, for spending time with me in Hong Kong. And to all of the other incredible humans in my life who continue to inspire and delight, prop me up and cheer me on. How lucky am I that there are too many of you to list? I know that you know who you are.

To my family, for making everything else possible: Mum, Dad, my split-apart twin Ben, Kathryn, Jack, Leif and Bear; my brother-from-another-mother Justin and family; Pop, the original Larsen poet; Nan, the original Larsen muse; Omi and Opi; Norma, Rob, Webley and Anne; our neiphlings and go(o)dchildren and the parents who gifted them to us; and all of our biological and logical families and friends all over the world. I love you all bigger than the sky.

And most of all, to Brien, for whom I will never have enough gratitude or words. Allsup. Always. Wherever you are is home.

Thank you.

FROM FREMANTLE PRESS

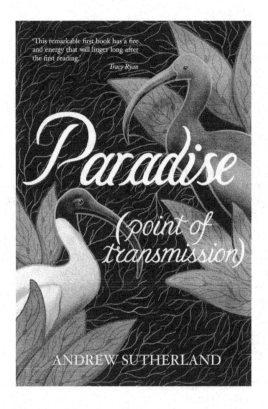

This brilliant debut collection examines a 'haunted' Queer and HIV-positive identity. It follows an HIV diagnosis and a departure from Singapore as the poet moves from concealing his HIV status towards a more public life, in which living openly with HIV is characterised by the queer longing toward both resilience and transformation.

AND ALL GOOD BOOKSTORES

First published 2023 by
FREMANTLE PRESS

Fremantle Press Inc. trading as Fremantle Press
PO Box 158, North Fremantle, Western Australia, 6159
fremantlepress.com.au

Cover image by Yuri Hoyda, Binary Code Chaos Wave, shutterstock.com/
image-vector/binary-code-chaos-wave-digital-technology-1417627217
Designed by Anna-Maley Fadgyas, bookdesigns.com.au
Printed and bound by IPG.

 A catalogue record for this
book is available from the
National Library of Australia

ISBN 9781760992163 (paperback)
ISBN 9781760992170 (ebook)

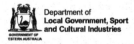

Fremantle Press is supported by the State Government through the
Department of Local Government, Sport and Cultural Industries.

Fremantle Press respectfully acknowledges the Whadjuk people of the
Noongar nation as the Traditional Owners and Custodians of the land
where we work in Walyalup.